WILD BILL HICKOK

LEGEND OF THE WILD WEST
LEYENDA DEL OESTE AMERICANO

LARISSA PHILLIPS

TRADUCCIÓN AL ESPAÑOL:
TOMÁS GONZÁLEZ

rosen central
Primary Source

Editorial Buenas Letras™

The Rosen Publishing Group, Inc., New York

Published in 2004 by The Rosen Publishing Group, Inc.
29 East 21st Street, New York, NY 10010

First Spanish Edition 2004
First English Edition 2004

Cataloging in Data

Phillips, Larissa.
[Wild Bill Hickok. Bilingual]
Wild Bill Hickok: Leyenda del oeste americano / Larissa Phillips.– 1st ed.
    p. cm. – (Primary sources of famous people in American history)
Summary: Profiles the life and exploits of William Hickok, the legendary Western sharpshooter known as Wild Bill.
Includes bibliographical references and index.
ISBN 0-8239-4170-1 (library binding)
1. Hickok, Wild Bill, 1837–1876—Juvenile literature. 2. Peace officers—West (U.S.)—Biography—Juvenile literature. 3. Frontier and pioneer life—West (U.S.)—Juvenile literature. 4. West (U.S.)—Biography–Juvenile literature. [1. Hickok, Wild Bill, 1837–1876. 2. Frontier and pioneer life—West (U.S.) 3. West (U.S.)—History—1860–1890. 4. Spanish Language Materials—Bilingual.]
I. Title. II. Series.: Primary sources of famous people in American history. Bilingual.
F594.H62P48 2004
978'.02'092—dc21

Manufactured in the United States of America

Photo credits: cover, pp. 5 (bottom), 11 (top) courtesy of Kansas State Historical Society; p. 5 (top) courtesy of Larissa Phillips; p. 7 Wilbur H. Siebert Collection, Archives of the Ohio Historical Society; 15, 23 Library of Congress Prints and Photographs Division; pp. 9, 11 (bottom), 13 Library of Congress Rare Book and Special Collections Division; p. 17 Courtesy of The Amon Carter Museum; p. 19 (top) New York Historical Society, New York, USA/Bridgeman Art Library; p. 19 (bottom) Library of Congress Geography and Map Division; pp. 21, 27 courtesy of Nebraska State Historical Society; p. 25 Buffalo Bill Historical Center, Cody, WY; p. 29 © Corbis.

Designer: Thomas Forget; Photo Researcher: Rebecca Anguin-Cohen

CONTENTS

CONTENIDO

1 THE BIRTH OF A SHARPSHOOTER

James Butler "Wild Bill" Hickok was born in Homer, Illinois, on May 27, 1837. He was the fifth child of William Alonzo Hickok and Polly Butler, a Vermont couple who married in 1829. The family moved west to Illinois in the 1830s.

---

1 NACIMIENTO DE UN TIRADOR EXTRAORDINARIO

James Butler Hickok, apodado "Wild Bill" (El Loco Bill), nació en Homer, Illinois, el 27 de mayo de 1837. Fue el quinto hijo de William Alonzo Hickok y Polly Butler, pareja de Vermont que se casó en 1829. En la década de 1830 la familia se mudó a Illinois.

William Alonzo Hickok, James's father, was born in Vermont in 1801.

William Alonzo Hickok, padre de James, nació en Vermont en 1801.

Polly Butler, a native of Vermont, married William Alonzo Hickok in 1829.

Polly Butler, natural de Vermont, se casó con William Alonzo Hickok en 1829.

The Hickok family members were pioneers who worked hard just to survive. They farmed and hunted for food. They made all their own clothes and furniture, and even their own soap. But they also helped runaway slaves escape. Helping slaves escape to safety was against the law.

———◆◆◆———

Los Hickok fueron colonizadores que trabajaban muy duro para sobrevivir. Obtenían sus alimentos por medio de la agricultura y la caza. Fabricaban sus propios vestidos y muebles, e incluso su propio jabón. Pero también ayudaban a escapar a esclavos fugitivos. Esto iba en contra de la ley.

UNITED STATES SLAVE TRADE.
1830.

This abolitionist print depicts the slave trade.

Este grabado abolicionista muestra el tráfico de esclavos.

At that time, slavery was legal in the United States. The Hickok family believed the law was wrong. These early experiences may have helped shape young James into the man he would become. Later known as Wild Bill, James Hickok is now one of the most famous men of the Wild West.

En esa época, la esclavitud era legal en Estados Unidos. La familia Hickok pensaba que la ley era injusta. Aquellas tempranas experiencias quizás ayudaron a que el joven James se convirtiera en el hombre que más tarde fue. Conocido después como "Wild Bill", James Hickok fue una de las personas más famosas del Lejano Oeste.

This image of a chained slave helped illustrate the poem "Our Countrymen in Chains," which recalled the horrors of slavery.

Esta imagen de un esclavo encadenado sirvió para ilustrar el poema "Nuestros compatriotas encadenados" sobre los horrores de la esclavitud.

2 HEADING WEST

There are many legendary stories about Wild Bill. For a few years, he wandered from job to job, always heading farther west. One such story claims that a bear attacked him. When his gun was knocked from his hands, he wrestled the bear to the ground and killed it with a knife.

---

2 RUMBO AL OESTE

Hay muchas leyendas sobre Wild Bill. Durante algunos años, cambiando siempre de trabajo, fue alejándose cada vez más hacia el oeste. En una de estas historias se cuenta que fue atacado por un oso. Cuando se le cayó el revólver de la mano, luchó cuerpo a cuerpo con el animal, lo derribó y lo mató con un cuchillo.

Above: Photograph of Abilene, Kansas, where Hickok was appointed U.S. marshal. *Below:* Depiction of one of the many stories that circulated about Hickok's life.

Arriba: Fotografía de Abilene, Kansas, donde Hickok fue nombrado alguacil del distrito. *Abajo:* Descripción de una de las numerosas historias que circularon sobre la vida de Hickok.

Another famous story claims that, in self-defense, Wild Bill was forced to kill nine men. Other people said that he killed only three men, and that he did it for fun. Perhaps that is when the name "Wild Bill" was born. Nobody knows for sure how a young pioneer became a sharpshooting legend of the Wild West.

En otra famosa historia se dice que Wild Bill se vio obligado a matar a nueve hombres en defensa propia. Algunos aseguraron que sólo había matado a tres y que lo hizo por diversión. Quizá fue entonces cuando se ganó el sobrenombre de "El Loco Bill". Nadie sabe con seguridad cómo el joven colonizador se convirtió en legendario tirador del Lejano Oeste.

Monthly.]   [Number. 3.

DE WITT'S TEN CENT ROMANCES

ONE

1867

Wild Bill, the Indian Slayer

FOR SALE BY
R. M. DE WITT, Publisher,
13 FRANKFORT STREET, N.Y.

This is the cover of the dime-store novel, *Wild Bill, the Indian Slayer*, which was one book that profiled his life in 1867.

Esta novela barata, *Wild Bill, el asesino de indios*, fue uno de los muchos libros que contaban la historia de su vida.

3   ARRESTED!

When the Civil War started in 1861, Wild Bill fought to abolish slavery. Soon the Confederate army arrested him for his actions. The soldiers tied him up and put him in a shack that served as a jail. They told him he would be shot in the morning.

---

3   ¡ARRESTADO!

En 1861, cuando comenzó la Guerra Civil, Wild Bill luchó por la abolición de la esclavitud. Muy pronto el ejército confederado lo arrestó por sus acciones. Los soldados lo ataron y lo metieron en una choza que hacía las veces de cárcel. Le dijeron que lo fusilarían en la mañana.

A group of Confederate soldiers in Charleston, South Carolina, during the Civil War

Un grupo de soldados confederados en Charleston, Carolina del Sur, durante la Guerra Civil

Wild Bill's situation seemed grim, but a glint of metal caught his eye. It was a knife! He used it to cut the ropes around his wrists and to kill the guard. In a fury, he took the guard's clothes and escaped.

La situación de Wild Bill parecía desesperada; sin embargo, un destello metálico atrajo su atención. ¡Se trataba de un cuchillo! Con él se liberó de las cuerdas que ataban sus muñecas y mató al guardia. Rápidamente se vistió con las ropas del guardia y escapó.

While he was a U.S. marshal, Wild Bill Hickok was persuaded to sit for this formal portrait by the photographer E. E. Henry.

Cuando Bill Hickok era alguacil, el fotógrafo E. E. Henry lo convenció de que posara para este retrato.

17

Two years after the Civil War ended in 1867, Wild Bill was appointed marshal, and then sheriff, of some of the roughest towns in Kansas. Then he was called to fight in the Indian wars. The settlers and the Native Americans were fighting over land.

———◆◆◆———

La Guerra Civil terminó en 1867 y, dos años después, Wild Bill fue nombrado alguacil, y luego sheriff, de algunos de los pueblos más violentos de Kansas. Luego lo llamaron para pelear en las llamadas "guerras indias" en las que los colonizadores y los nativos americanos peleaban por la tierra.

Above: A depiction of an attack on Native Americans at the Tippecanoe River. *Below:* This map illustrates the industrial developments in Kansas City, Missouri, around 1871.

Arriba: Descripción del ataque contra los indios en el río Tippecanoe.
Abajo: Este mapa ilustra el desarrollo industrial de Kansas City en 1871.

4 WILD BILL, THE SHOWMAN

During the Indian wars, Wild Bill acted as a guide and a dispatch rider for General George Custer. To avoid being killed by Native Americans, he disguised himself and traveled by night.

---

4 WILD BILL, EL ARTISTA

Durante las guerras indias, Wild Bill sirvió de guía y de jinete mensajero del general George Custer. Para que los indios no lo mataran, se disfrazaba y viajaba por la noche.

Wild Bill's appearance in this picture suggests that it was taken during his time as a showman (1872–1873).

El aspecto de Wild Bill en esta fotografía sugiere que fue tomada durante su época de artista (1872–1873).

By the end of the Indian wars, Wild Bill was famous. It was said that if someone threw a coin in the air, Wild Bill could shoot a hole in it. For a year, he starred in Buffalo Bill's Wild West show. But Wild Bill did not enjoy the life of a showman. He soon headed back to the real Wild West.

———◆———

Al terminar las guerras indias, Wild Bill era famoso. Se decía que si alguien lanzaba una moneda al aire, Wild Bill podía hacerle un agujero de un disparo. Durante un año actuó en el espectáculo del Lejano Oeste, de Buffalo Bill. Pero a Wild Bill no le agradaba la vida del espectáculo y muy pronto regresó al verdadero oeste.

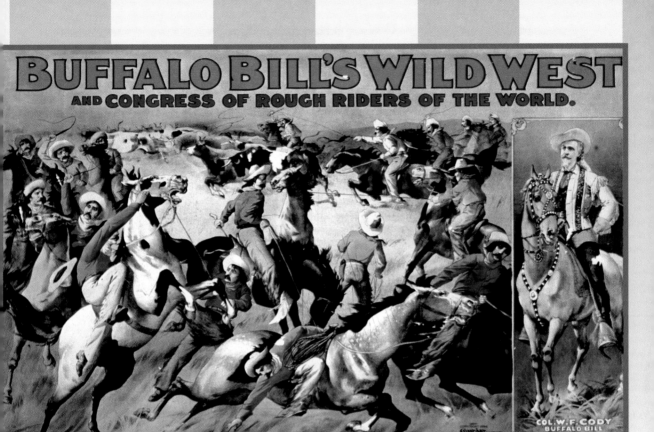

Advertisement poster for Buffalo Bill's Wild West show (1899)

Cartel del espectáculo del Lejano Oeste de Buffalo Bill (1899)

5 THE DEATH OF A LEGEND

Wild Bill always said he would die with his boots on, and he was right. In 1876, Wild Bill headed for Deadwood, South Dakota, to mine for gold. Deadwood was a wild town, often plagued by barroom brawls that ended with gunshots. Wild Bill, who loved to gamble, felt right at home.

---

5 MUERTE DE UNA LEYENDA

Wild Bill siempre dijo que moriría con las botas puestas, y así fue. En 1876 se dirigió a Deadwood, Dakota del Sur, en busca de oro. Deadwood era un pueblo violento, donde a menudo se producían riñas en los bares que terminaban a tiros. Wild Bill, que amaba el juego, se sintió como en casa.

Wild Bill Hickok *(left)*, **Texas Jack Omohundro** *(center)*, **and Buffalo Bill Cody** *(right)*.

Wild Bill Hickok *(izquierda)*, Texas Jack Omohundro *(centro)* y Buffalo Bill Cody *(derecha)*.

One afternoon in 1876, Wild Bill was playing poker in a place called Saloon Number 10. A man named John McCall arrived and shot him in the back of the head. The people in the saloon caught McCall and brought him to justice.

***

Una tarde de 1876, Wild Bill jugaba póker en un bar llamado *Saloon Number 10*. Llegó un hombre llamado John McCall y le disparó en la parte posterior de la cabeza. La gente que había en el bar atrapó a McCall y lo entregó a la justicia.

The last known photograph of Wild Bill Hickok, likely taken in 1875

Última fotografía conocida de Wild Bill Hickok, probablemente en 1875

Today it's hard to know the truth about Wild Bill. He fought against slavery. But he also fought to push Native Americans off land that had been theirs for years and years. He claimed he had shot men only to defend himself, though others claimed he was a cold-blooded killer. It is certain, however, that Wild Bill was a true Western legend.

Es difícil saber la verdad sobre Wild Bill. Luchó contra la esclavitud pero también luchó para expulsar a los indios de sus tierras. Decía que sólo había matado a otros en defensa propia, pero algunos aseguraban que era un asesino a sangre fría. Sea como sea, no hay duda de que Wild Bill fue una verdadera leyenda del Oeste.

Cowgirl Calamity Jane (Martha Jane Cannary) standing by Wild Bill's grave

La vaquera Calamity Jane (Martha Jane Cannary) de pie junto a la tumba de Wild Bill

TIMELINE

1837—On May 27 James Butler "Wild Bill" Hickok is born.

1861—Now known as Wild Bill, Hickok joins the Union army as the Civil War begins.

1867—During the 1867 Indian war, Hickok is appointed U.S. marshal.

1869—Wild Bill kills several men.

1873—Wild Bill stars in Buffalo Bill's Wild West Show.

1876—Five months after his marriage to Agnes Lake Thatcher, Wild Bill is shot dead in a saloon.

CRONOLOGÍA

1837—El 27 de mayo nace James Butler "Wild Bill" Hickok.

1861—Conocido ahora como Wild Bill, Hickok se une al ejército de la Unión al comenzar la Guerra Civil.

1867—Durante la guerra de 1867 contra los indios, Hickok es nombrado alguacil.

1869—Wild Bill mata a varios hombres.

1873—Se presenta en el espectáculo del Lejano Oeste, de Buffalo Bill.

1876—Cinco meses después de casarse con Agnes Lake Thatcher, Wild Bill es asesinado de un disparo en un bar.

GLOSSARY

abolitionist (a-buh-LIH-shun-ist) A person who worked to end slavery.

brawl (BRALL) A rough fight.

dispatch rider (DIS-PACH RY-der) A soldier who carriers important messages from officer to officer.

legend (LEJ-uhnd) A person who has many stories told about him or her. Sometimes the stories may not be true.

pioneers (PY-uh-NEERZ) Some of the first people to settle in a new area.

settlers (SET-lerz) People who move to a new land to live.

WEB SITES

Due to the changing nature of Internet links, the Rosen Publishing Group, Inc., has developed an online list of Web sites related to the subject of this book. This site is updated regularly. Please use this link to access the list:

http://www.rosenlinks.com/fpah/wbhi

GLOSARIO

abolicionista (el, la) Persona que luchó por acabar con la esclavitud.

colonizadores (los) Personas que se establecen en una nueva región.

jinete mensajero (el, la) Soldado que lleva mensajes importantes de unos oficiales a otros.

leyenda (la) Historia que pasa de generación en generación y no puede ser probada.

pioneros (los) Personas que inician la exploración de un nuevo territorio.

riña (la) Altercado violento.

SITIOS WEB

Debido a las constantes modificaciones en los sitios de Internet, Rosen Publishing Group, Inc., ha desarrollado un listado de sitios Web relacionados con el tema de este libro. Este sitio se actualiza con regularidad. Por favor, usa este enlace para acceder a la lista:

http://www.rosenlinks.com/fpah/wbhi

INDEX

ABOUT THE AUTHOR

Larissa Phillips is a writer living in Brooklyn, New York.

ÍNDICE

ACERCA DEL AUTOR

Larissa Phillips es escritora. Vive en Brooklyn, Nueva York.